A Petroglyph of His Own Choosing

BY

Benjamin A. Kerner

LinCom PRESS, Maple City, Michigan

A PETROGLYPH OF HIS OWN CHOOSING.

ACKNOWLEDGEMENTS:

For permission to quote a portion of James Wright's poem, "Father," from *Above the River, The Complete Poems,* copyright © 1990 by Anne Wright. Reprinted by permission of The New England University Press.

For permssion to use the photograph of the author, as shown on the back cover, copyright © 1997 by Olan Mills.

Cover design and illustration, copyright © 1997 by Lightbourne Images.

Library of Congress Catalogue Card Number: 97-74604.

ISBN 0-9658945-0-9

Printed in the United States of America.

9 8 7 6 5 4 3 2 1

Published by: LinCom PRESS
11822 South Tower Rd.
Maple City, Michigan

DEDICATION

With Love to my Dad,
Edward H. Kerner

In paradise I poised my foot above the boat and said:
Who prayed for me?
. . . who is waiting?
. . . .
It was my father wandering round the waters at the wharf.

James Wright, "Father,"
from *Above the River, The Complete Poems.*

APPRECIATIONS

- To my wife, Denyce, for her steadiness, support and love.

- To my daughter, Nicole, for being herself, and for untangling my computer files.

- To my publisher, Linda Sioen, who had the sense to see a gem in the rough and the energy to give it all her considerable polish.

CONTENTS

INTRODUCTION

Every poet has his or her special niche of perception and a translation mechanism to read out the feelings that go with internal and external perceptions. My niche is partially defined by the ambiguity I see and feel in many quotidian occurrences. French painter Georges Braque elevated this ambiguity to a high esthetic, attempting with due deliberateness to play on the ambiguity he saw and felt in his day, in his world of renaissance Paris of the post-World War I era. He found an expression for his esthetic which has endured and enchanted knowledgeable observers. In a still life, for instance, he managed at once to suggest the life-giving form of a female; while in the subtext of the use of sand and found-objects on the canvas, he also conveyed a profound sense of stasis, the earthbound stillness of vase and flowers and fish on the table. Braque called his esthetic one of "metamorphosis." One image can be and can represent several different objects, feeling states, and even different denotational subjects.

I have adopted the same esthetic. But in my case, the ambiguity of my approach to language is heightened by the fact that I am professionally trained as a lawyer. I earn my living by being quintessentially neat, clear, and, at all costs, unambiguous in the denotations of the words used in a contract, in interpreting a statute, or (as in my main business of arbitrating disputes) in understanding someone else's contract and interpolating its meaning in a (usually) unforeseen factual situation. Thus, as I ply the trades of lawyer and arbitrator, I utilize the training all good lawyers have in understanding and in representing reality with words that correspond one-to-one with the reality which they are intended to represent.

Yet, thoughtful lawyers know that the doctrine of unambiguous expression is a necessary fiction: We always bring to the understanding of language the culture, the context, the training, the relational history that we know to exist, whether or not it is expressed in the language under scrutiny at the present time. We know that, even if these contextual elements are expressed in some way, they cannot *all* be expressed. The reader must supply some of the missing elements.

In plying my craft as a poet I find that the contextual elements of written and spoken language loom large. They are an explicit part of the poem, just as Braque's sand and newspaper clippings from the Paris *Figaro* are an explicit part of his art. It is the business of poets, after all, to shake things up by supplying new meanings in old contexts; to take a word with known reference points and connotations, and by the phrase in which it is placed suggest altogether new connotations. By giving known quantities such new, unexpected meanings we effect implicit metaphors. It is one of the great and beautiful things that we wordsmiths can do.

Consider, for example: "The force that through the green fuse drives the flower." (Dylan Thomas). Or:

> (Her big and firm legs) . . .
> remind me of Woman and
> how between
> her hips India is
> ("my small headed pearshaped,"
> e.e. cummings)

It is from such implicit metaphors that the "ah-ha" shock of recognition and new understanding arises.

How far can we go with such implicit metaphors? A few poets, William Carlos Williams, e.e. cummings, and Wallace Stevens, were masters of implicit metaphor. Many readers cannot follow their metaphors. I cannot follow many good poets to their cosmic hiding places. But I have noticed that the use of traditional structures, by providing a recognizable context to the new content, sometimes helps immeasurably, sometimes helps you follow. I hope through the device of traditional poetic structures–the sonnet, the villanelle, pentameter quatrains, traditional rhyming patterns–to acquaint you with my implicit metaphors and the music they make.

The far away places of the poetic mind have much in common with the jazz musician's scanning and creation of the musical line. Listen to Ella. Listen to Louis Armstrong. What are they talking about when they scat a tune? You can hear all kinds of words. You can hear all kinds of sounds not recognizably words. You can feel strong, well-defined emotions listening to those songs. Where do these feelings come from? From the feeling of the songster, evidently, made plain and palpable in the structure of the blues.

Thus, I don't worry too much if someone bright and literate and cultured says to me, "I don't understand that poem. I like the feeling you convey; but I can't understand what it's about." The feeling **is** what it's about. Plus, the love of the Great Lakes. The love of the ever-changing weather. The love of being in it, between the deep blue sky and the devil in the sea. The love of women; and the peace I've found in loving Denyce, my wife and loyal friend, leaving me in awe for the first time in my long and arduous career as a lover that few can be more.

I love the feeling of connectedness that comes from seeing drawings 10,000 years old on the "greenstone" walls of the Canadian shield, where Potawatomi and Ottawa Indians tread gently; carried big sticks; dreamed their dreams for the future and consulted their forebears, as we can only dimly tell when we see their drawings, petroglyphs, high above our fiberglass canoes. I love the feeling of connectedness that comes from being middle-aged, and having lost some capacities while developing others; having lost some family while developing other intimacies. And, isn't it true that we word-crazy people ultimately love the feeling of connectedness to the words, to the way it brings us out of ourselves–out for you, the reader, but also out of our egotistical burdened selves, to dance with the nymphs and the trolls and the elves of legend.

Enjoy, dear reader, the ambiguity is meant for you!

THE ROOKERY

AMSTERDAM

To Bregje

Reeking green canals
and stately burgher mansions
crossed by squealing trams
and crowded avenues
on stakes and stout arcades
are crossed by tourist cruisers,
garbage, fruit, or flower barges.

Eyes like great green parks
a lonely man could stroll in,
spy upon though never
overtake her heart,
there play a children's game
of love and wonder if
a feeling hope will take it home.

Those times, old Amsterdam, her eyes;
the fantasy, her eyes, the passion
I will I won't remember.

PORTRAIT OF A LADY

Not lovely, charming, sweet, nor homely, unmanned
Innocent she sparkles at the party
Though her guests are unaware of it
Until they've left: her wit is in her laughter,
Smiles; the turning word is lifted on
The way she walks, the curve of eyebrow. Once
Her carriage or the gentle humor of
Her upturned lips impelled a man to pro-
Testations of his love; but others pass
Her by remarking on her grace. She is
Not captivating, elegant; not dull,
Nor plain: a singularly simple girl.

WINTER LOCAL

A shrug of settled steel melts indifference
In the waiting room: a rush of rails
Gives some purpose to the lonesome, lost
Profundity of falling snow. The train
Comes trembling to a halt. "All aboard."
A second muffled shudder and she's lost
Within the earth-and-sky-and-God encircling
Wall of white. Two blinkers tick: a clock.

Past sleeping freight yards, meditating boxcars,
Engines brooding on their soon demise;
Past frozen fields in a priestly guise;
On shivering wires, chattering tracks; past slums
And graveyards, vacant buildings moves the train:
A lonely pilgrim in the holy snow.

GEORGES BRAQUE

A poetry of texture, music
Wrought in visual counterpoint
The point which frames the canvas joins
The artist to his eye: Georges Braque
Is caught in self-illuminating
Lines beyond our point of view.

A metaphor that reads both ways to freedom
as a table leg shaped to a woman;
or a tone as simple as a lute
like marbletop or paper-patterned walls,
A frozen bird, *le jour* as centerpiece;
A broken mandolin, a seated nude . . . .

So goes the play on matter: work
Of winds is twice told always and
Imagination draws from double
Chaos this: a cosmos. Braque
who paints gives shape to all creation
on the finger of his mind.

TWO BROTHERS: THOMAS

Three years old: a beast with blinking eyes
makes monster to your face; but disbelieve him
or make faces back and he will cry
until you hold him close and cuddle him.

The bully on a block of older knocking kids
he even hits his older scolding brother
'til his playmate knocks **him** in the head;
then bully breaks for babe and rainy weather.

Playing indoors on account of storm
he listens for the lightning, waits for thunder's
bump upon the window; makes a storm
of squeaks and squawks, and squeals of wonder.

Tom-Tom's a scalawag, brash and blustering,
hard as a barnacle attached to mother ship
yet soft as clam meat, unformed as a jellyfish
he is a seashell not yet rolled in the roll of the sea.

ANDREW

Five years old and playing by himself,
Andrew makes a chorus of his voice,
to commentate upon his talking play
(a Greek interpretation of his choice.)

Which is no choice since he is inwardly
alone and knows to multiply himself
to make him company: he orchestrates
a playable ensemble of his little self.

Tears at any moment from an onslaught
of his bully brother, sensitive
to people as he is to poison ivy
shrouded in the underbrush of life,

Andrew is a youngster antelope not yet sure
of his natural gait and pace (to come in time);
tenderly he chews the shoots while roaming
in the garden which his parents grow.

POEM

Long-limbed and thin of flesh she spins the darkness
In her arms: her kisses resonate
Beyond the flicking lips, the twisting tongue;
Her fingers lift uncertainty above
The fitful counterfeit of love. A lilac
Fragrance and its pattern on her thighs
Will couch the cradle of our age. And time-
Unshedding breasts confirm the ticking flesh
Which otherwise is sealed inside the clock.

ON A MONDAY

In midwinter town
they drove me to the train
and going home I found
that snow is just the same
and falling everyplace.
What more is there to say?

Say, have you ever noticed
how an all-day snowfall
rounds all corners though it
sharpens up the air?
An old man in the same coach noted this:
"We're going through . . ." though I forget just where.

ANNIE

("Annie," Apollinaire)

On the sea-coast of Texas
Near Mobile, near Galveston
Roses are blooming
A garden of roses,
And the house a big rose.

A woman walks often—alone
In the garden where I on the lime-
Bordered road often pass—we each look . . . .

A Mennonite woman she is
Her rosebush, her clothes have no buttons;
My vest lacks two of the same.
The lady and I share one rite.

WHITE SNOW

("La Blanche Neige," Apollinaire)

Angels, angels in the sky
One is dressed like an officer,
And one is clothed like a cook.
The rest are singing.

Handsome sky blue officer
The spring long after Christmas time
Will pin a sun on you,
A handsome sun.

The cook is plucking geese.
Ah snow is falling
Falling and
My love is far from me.

AUTUMN

("L'autumne," Apollinaire)

In the fog plod a peasant—he's hobbling along
With his ox—very slowly in autumn' s gray fog
Which hides the poor village, humble and dumb.

The peasant in passing will murmur a song
A song about love—and a love never gathered,
A song of a ring and a heart that is shattered.

Oh autumn, oh autumn has brought summer's wane.
In a mist plod two silhouettes—tattered and gray.

MIRABEAU BRIDGE

("Le Pont Mirabeau," Apollinaire)

Under Mirabeau Bridge flows the Seine
And I my loves
Remember again
But joy with sadness usually tends.

Call the night, ring the day;
So time must go and I must stay.

Hand in hand, nose to nose
Beneath the bridge
Our figures make, the slow
Eternal waves of looking flow.

Call the night, ring the day;
So time must go and I must stay.

Love like running water runs
Love always sprints
Life slowly goes and comes;
And hope, the least of hope, can stun.

Call the night, ring the day;
So time must go and I must stay.

Days pass; and weeks must come to end
Not time gone past
Nor love returns again;
Under Mirabeau Bridge flows the Seine.

Call the night, ring the day;
So time must go and I must stay.

MY STRANGE RECURRING DREAM

("Mon Reve Familier," Paul Verlaine)

I often dream a strange, a potent dream
About an unknown woman whom I love,
A woman who each night is not the one
She was nor quite another; and who loves me,
Understand she does; my heart, which beats
For her alone, resolves its only question
And for her alone; the fever of
My aging brow is waning as she weeps.

But is she red-head, brunette, or a blond?
I do not know. Her name? I recollect
It rhymes with those of loved-ones life has banished.
When she sings, the sirens hold their song;
And her distant, calming voice reflects
The rhythm of loved voices which are vanished.

POEM

Wet snow crackles on old oak
leaves; the auditory nerve is tickled
by the touch and so the old parade
of nervous starts is marshaled on the page.
It only happens only after
many missaphors and moons
when more stupendous noise and efforts
couldn't order the attention.
Wet snow crackling on oak leaves says:
Let snow be you, dude poet, sir, and oak leaves
be the leavings of a stale season.
Wet snow crackles on old oak leaves, then.

POEM FOR MY FATHER

A physicist and true-born man
If stranded on some desert land
Would write equations in the sand.
The moon's obliterating hand
Would wash his work: It still would stand.

WINIFRED,

Do you remember how at five
You lead the moon through exercises
On a string; or did it dance
And pull you with it that you ran?
A moonstring ties the heavens to this earth.

TO BARBARA
On Her 50th Birthday

To play the cello
like a fellow
who has felt it
from the womb
will take more years
of practice, I assume,
than writing tunes
on birthday runes
but not so many years
of patience and of low
returns as was demanded
of the craftsman
in fashioning the cello.

become and bewildered upon this glowing planet,
born to live outside, cropping the stars
(as you lie down to sleep) with ancient myths and modern
dreams no boy has ever dreamt so far;
when you are old, you'll know those dreams may tarnish
but the rubbing power in their ancient light survives
to etch a portrait of your jawbone, large
and weighty, frozen against the jabbering jive.

Now that I'm older, just a little bit older, still
I love to lie head northward in the summer sky
and watch bright Perseid's fire glinting from her thundering
thighs, racing downward, dreamward, winding
low upon the hill. I dream no boy
has gone to the hill without remembering this joy.

SEPTEMBER SCENES: A SUITE

I.
chalk dust and coal smoke
where ragweed and the bitch summer's heat
rode the air.

II.
never, reads the kiss of friendship
and dry willows wash
the swift creek bed.

III.
a southern sunlight
plays the veins;
bloodlit from the touch,
my numbers jump.

IV.
where are you
dare to be
don't ever doubt
said South Street
singing the blues.

V.
walls of glass
inside
two of the newer students
nipping in the grass.

VI.
down the ocean limps
a leaf and like sleep
every steeple floats a cloud.

VII.
in Rome
do as
the Romans do,
except,
of course,
they take account of you.

VIII.
then spins the distant fall
within my ears
faint, like the roar of a train.

IX.
You, say You,
why did you plant the notion
that my toga wraps the root?

X.
my breath, a ghost, same way's
this poem, this century, or
the Milky Way.

CROSSCUTS

(with apologies to William Carlos Williams)

I.
The big blue sweater breast girl
unwheeling down the street
turns, stops, takes her newspaper off
and smiles at the man
who passes her, eyes down.

II.
In the car between me and the sunset
someone young and handsome
strokes his throat, revealing
a cool close shave, relaxed
and ready to engorge the night.

III.
Half past twelve and all is well
with little boy's big hands
inside his goyle's half-unbuttoned blouse.
He flounders with the buckle at her back
at last uncatching it
and all is well at half-past twelve.

IV.
Like a Degas dancer at his best
my little urchin sitting on the beach
unclasps her hair
and stretches out to feel the sun
with one hand dabbling at her ample breast;
then scratches at her unflared backside,
caught in the crosscut of time through my eyes.

SOUTHERN SKY AT MIDNIGHT

Poetry is no match for love:
for love has its own meaning
but poetry has no warmth, no glow
except when lined with feeling.

Simple lust is more alive
than matching words to love:
it's effortless and everywhere,
even in the stars above.

One winter night I walked alone
away from love's warm paws;
from nowhere came the hard-earned truth.
Then toward the South I saw

the mangy lion rear his head
beneath the virgin's thighs
and sigh how he is always chasing
after her pie in the sky.

ROCK FORMATIONS

MAY I HAVE THIS DANCE?

When we met we were both ripe for some new experiences. Janine had in mind to learn the fine points of ballroom dance. I had never danced in my life, having grown up on a family that scorned the social graces. We enrolled in dance class at the Middle School, and went every Tuesday religiously at 7:00 p.m. That was a hot summer, sticky and muggy in the airless gym. Susan, our class instructor, demonstrated the rumba, the waltz, the fox trot, the swing, and we all dutifully went through the basic steps. I remember holding Janine limpidly, and looking over her shoulder at other more beautiful women. We learned all the basic steps, and we learned to hold one another in basic dance position, and to feel comfortable dancing those basic steps.

At the end of the evening we stopped for ice cream on the way to her house. We ate on the sidewalk terrace, in the old restored Depot Town. We talked a blue streak, me about my failed marriage, she, in reassuring terms about the parallel experiences she had had. We developed rapport in our style, in our listening ability, in the flow of our conversation.

Then one day sitting in her driveway, late at night, as the talk continued, she leaned over and put her hand on my crotch. I was excited, but I had not wanted to make a move with this paragon of Southern virtue and I was in no mood anyway for a sexual involvement with any woman. But her single hand motion broke through my reserve, and in a week's time we were into bed.

By the end of the summer we felt confident enough of our dance styling to try a regular dance floor. We went to a club featuring single people and live dance music. I found that I liked to dance with the other available women, many of whom were there strictly to meet men. Of course, they were good dancers, and I found that I liked leading them, liked ogling them, and liked making an occasional date for coffee. On those occasions I went out with every expectation of making a full-fledged conquest. But before it got to a Saturday night date, I realized that I would be letting the air out of my new-found relationship with Janine to make a date with a new woman for a Saturday night. So I left it at coffee and maybe one week-night out for dinner. Then, at the next dance club session, I would dance with abandon, but explain that I had a regular lady and was not free to date.

I dated Janine steadily, and found that we enjoyed all sorts of activities besides dancing. Our talk, now shifting from my former marriage to our present relationship, got richer; and we both talked more freely of our past, the distant past of family closeness and family disabilities. We began to understand each other's psychological workings and needs. However, I never quite understood her deep and continuing need for visible and vocalized attention. If she ran low on that score, she was inclined to do the craziest things, including going out for a date with another man on the spur of the moment.

We danced throughout the next year, mainly at the Tuesday night single's club. We continued in the pattern of dancing with one another for a few sets, and reserving a few sets to dance with the strangers, or in her case, with the older men who lavished attention on her. Several of those brought back things from their travels, and several of those men must have told her in no uncertain terms what a beauty she was and what a fine dancer, and who knows what other flatteries. I just danced with her. Sometimes she began to state how she would like to dance every dance with me. I simply ignored that remark, and continued to reserve several dances each evening for dances with strange women. I even continued to make an occasional date for coffee. All to no avail.

We also traveled an hour's drive on a Saturday evening to attend the open-air dance at Palisades Terrace. That was a special place. A floor the size of half a football field, made of three foot square marble tiles, joined seamlessly to create a smooth capacious surface. Sometimes fifty couples would be dancing at one time, wide Venetian style waltzes. And you could dance to the far end of the floor, move through the whole line of dance back to the front, and never be within arm's reach of another couple. In one circuit of the floor you might cover the time needed for one dance.

We had now become good dancers, at least in certain dances, such as the waltz and the cha-cha. We relished the flare and ability we displayed. And we were not afraid to try some new steps, right in the open air, under the stars, for all to see. By then, we had become self-confident as dancers and as a couple. We knew each other's ways, we knew one another's moves, and we enjoyed holding and letting go, in the sure knowledge that we could always complete the turn, rejoin the basic dance step and hold each other lovingly in a definite and comfortable posture.

This sense of self-confidence and comfort continued for most of the next two years. We became true intimates. We developed love and affection for one another. And our dancing became all the smoother, all the more seamless.

Then, by the end of the third summer, something strange affected our dancing. I had noticed, on each occasion from the very beginning of our relationship, that every time the band played a song called, "May I have this dance, For the rest of your life?" that Janine's eyes swelled, and she looked at me longingly. I never responded verbally, but I enjoyed holding her tightly through that dance. We took extra turns, and both relished the flow, the smooth beauty of that song, especially as played by the Johnnie Knorr orchestra at the Palisades. I didn't think verbal response was necessary. It was.

She wanted to be married. I had not really given the matter any serious thought. We talked about it jokingly, and we talked about the accompaniments of marriage such as finding a house. But we never talked about getting married.

After a few months, when she saw that I had no present interest in the subject, she began to get restless. She began to take an interest in another man, very quietly, in fact so quietly that I knew nothing about it. Just another friend at the office. Then, she announced that she felt there was something wrong with our relationship, and that she would have to go her separate way. I was thunderstruck. I was devastated. Our plans, not fully verbalized as marriage plans, but verbalized sufficiently to be couple-plans for the future, were knocked into a cocked hat. My sense of comfort with the only woman I had known to be reliably there, and reliably capable of listening to me, was shattered. The relationship was over.

On our last outing to the Palisades, we were getting ready to leave when the band struck up, "May I have this dance, For the rest of your life?" By then Janine had gone to the women's room. I was left alone on the edge of the floor, wondering with whom I might ever dance this dance again. She returned and we danced the last chorus, slightly in a hurry, slightly out-of-step. We said good-night to the Palisades.

SKIING WITH A NEWCOMER

When we took our first trip skiing—to the Thumb of Michigan—it turned out to be ice-cold with a bitter damp wind chilling the air; and a frozen ice trail. At the beginning of the season in Michigan, the conditions are highly variable from one locale to another: on this December weekend, there was no fresh snow on the East side of the state, but lots of fresh powder on the Traverse-Mancelona-Gaylord Western tier of the state. We had chosen the wrong venue.

But we were there and determined to make the best of it. Janine rented sleek racing skis, much to my chagrin. Janine was then a newcomer to skiing. She needed solid dependable touring skis to get the feel of the trail: to learn foot control; to gain confidence in her ability to turn and stop. Away we went, however, in the setting sun of a Friday afternoon with no fresh powder under foot, but lots of enthusiasm under hat.

The trail winds gently uphill along the first half of the loop following the edge of dense pine woods. Janine was not attuned to the technique of climbing hills, even small grade hills, on cross country skis. I kept waxing and re-waxing her skis, trying stickier skid wax, then klister. Finally I showed her the old technique of jumping side-to-side, putting all one's weight on the holding ski, just before the glide: then shifting all one's weight with a bump to the sliding ski, just as it stops. She found that worked well, bumping along, side-to-side with all 125 pounds of her little body shifting dramatically from one ski to the other. At the top of the loop she was breathing hard: frost-breath clouded the air between us. But she was smiling!

I suppose I'm a fool for taking the chance of acquainting a newcomer with a sport as fine-tuned as skiing and doing so in the worst of conditions. I took the fool's chance.

On the back half of the loop going through the pine woods, there were more and more patches of better-preserved snow. Every so often, there was a patch of sheer ice underneath a half-inch coating of powder snow, left over from yesterday's dusting. We both slipped and skidded, unsure how to regain control on ice. She took a brief spill or two. She always got up quickly, not even taking time to dust off, and resumed her stride.

Toward the bottom of the loop, having been out on the trail all of an hour, she was beginning to get the feel of the glide stroke. Her natural body rhythm found a way of absorbing the clumsy impediment of the skis and she was beginning to direct them, with the control from the knees that is so necessary to the sport of skiing.

We stayed at the Holiday Inn, and rested awhile in our room. There is nothing like the bliss of a hot shower after a long (or a short) ski. And being away from home added pizzazz to the mix. After a shower, there is nothing so blissful as making love with the one you care for, in quiet and relaxed unscheduled peace. Late in the evening, we went down to eat. The hostess, sensing our lovers' aura, placed us in a corner table, away from the hubbub of the main serving area. We ate a dinner which I can still remember. But the details would bore the reader. I suppose it was the looking and the talking that were special, not the food.

Next day we skied some more, and this day we were blessed with a little overnight powder. As the day unfolded I felt Janine taking more and more command of her skis. She was a natural. She was egging me on, asking for more challenging trails. We crossed the road, and tried the advanced loop. She struggled a little, but kept her feet, and kept her stride. Her skill, for a first time skier, was impressive.

The whiteness and the cleanness of the snow is one of the reasons cross-country skiers go into the woods. There is something unspoiled and child-like beautiful in the fresh snow, glistening off the pine boughs. In major downfall areas, the snow makes sculptures, incredible wind-blown figurines hanging precariously off the fallen limbs and tree trunks. In a spruce or balsam fir woods, the snow drops off the limbs, and holds only if the temperature is near the freezing mark. In Eastern pine woods, the five long tentacles of the needle-bundles hold the snow and weight the branches down. Even a light fresh snow can build up great reserves of bundled snow. In the bright sunlight, fresh snow in an Eastern pine woods dazzles the senses, with little sparkles of prismatic light dancing at you every way you turn.

One day melded into the next. We retreated to our room only when we were exhausted. Then we made love at great length. And didn't feel exhausted. One night we watched a rather forgettable unforgettable movie about people who die in strange and premature ways, then come back as ghosts. Their ghosts haunt the perpetrators, the drunken drivers and witless husbands. In our overly excited state, these scenes could only be described as surreal. They were so unnatural that we laughed. The movie was not intended to be funny. But we were laughing up a storm.

Then, on the day of departure, we packed huge full-sized suitcases, suitable for a 2-week trip to France. (Ski gear is capacious.) I toted it out to the car. Janine brought our coffee-thermos to the car. We were ready and loaded. An old habit of my mother's appealed to me at that instant. I went back to the motel room, for a final check: one doesn't want to leave a sock or a mitten or a treasured earring under the bed or next to the TV. Janine followed. The door closed, and with heat high, we fell into one another's arms on the bed; in two seconds we had our clothes off. And furious passionate love-making we made.

As far as the Holiday Inn was concerned, we were checked out. The maid was on her way. The new guests could be arriving within the hour.

But we had our way, with no second thoughts and no regrets. The rest of the trip home was an easy glide downhill from there.

MEETING MY BROTHER

Once, intending to visit the Museum of Fine Arts in Boston, I waited for a trolley with my father for the long ride to the Fenway. We stood chatting for a few minutes in the late autumn fine shaded sun; then the trolley came, ricketing down Commonwealth Avenue, singing the screech of the rails, clanging to a sudden stop. We boarded the old orange and yellow museum piece. My brother was seated on the left seat, just behind the driver. Jeff lived at that time in Providence, and had come to Boston for the day expressly to see the same Van Gogh exhibit which we were headed to see. Dad lit up, Jeff smiled the wan, impassive grin of the deeply, inwardly depressed. He had on a light lumber jacket, although the air was cool and the forecast was for rain.

What did the weather forecast mean to him? He had his inner weather to contend with. He didn't see the clear blue sky or the threatening low-scudding stratus clouds. He rode in his own weather. He sat on the trolley seat, for all the world like a novitiate, waiting, listening, watching for the master to speak to him.

I greeted Jeff, too, surprised and delighted that chance could place us on the same trolley, in the same city, going to see the same exhibit on a bright weekend afternoon. We rode to the Museum and saw the Van Gogh exhibit. We marveled at the day's new canvases, those not known to us from prior excursions, beginning with a family outing to the Albright Knox Gallery in Buffalo a dozen years ago. I thought then, after study of the art books, that I was familiar with all of Van Gogh's major paintings. The distorted blaring vision of the master was known to me through and through. But here at a new exhibit I found that there were several major paintings—the church in Paris and the boats at Arles—that I didn't know. What a surprise, to see the new manifestation of the old vision. And, then, the perennial surprise of seeing again the familiar pieces, the Potato Eaters, the Abycinth Drinker, the Room at Arles—again to feel the fresh rush of impulsively laid paint, the power of the deep-forgotten inner view.

We each had moments of gawking and moments of surprise. We enjoying being there together, the three men of our family, the progenitor, and the two sons. We knew we belonged together. We knew we belonged together from long ago, perhaps a score of years ago, when we went hiking down the beach on Long Island. We took our dinner in a knapsack; waded across Wading River, and found the tide had come up to armpit level when we wanted to reclaim a camping spot on the near side of the River. We slept in the open air—no tent—on the cold hard beach. We talked of things kids are interested in. We talked about the stars, Dad describing the way in which stars keep shining. I was interested in the patterns that they make and later learned all the Northern constellations. Jeff was interested in the chemistry of their fusion machines.

Then, at the start of the new day we threw off all sleeping bags and tarps and caution, and dove into the gentle waves, delighting in the primeval cold, and shivering from the short hairs to the scalp. But what a day: we frolicked, all of us, like the kids we were.

In Boston, the Museum closing time arrived. We had feasted on every painting in the gallery. We had gone back to see several of the master's paintings twice and three times. The green-gray Museum corridors led us to the Fenway, cold and green and gray with simply falling rain.

Beyond the visit to the Museum, I'm not precisely sure how the day ended. I think we went to get a bite to eat at a submarine shop. On the way, walking to wherever we went, Jeff stopped to hitch up the waist corset he was wearing to steady a failed back. He did this artlessly and innocently, half unbuckling his belt and shifting his weight and stuffing his hands inside his pants, right there on the side of the street. He missed a few beats, slowing his steady gait, so that when Dad and I turned around, he had his pants half undone, and was completing the job.

The day done, the happenstance complete, Jeff got on a trolley to South Station and returned to Providence. Dad and I returned to my apartment, delighted at such a brief encounter. We had dinner in the glow of that serendipitous meeting, that reuniting of the men of our family.

Years later, after Jeff was gone, I thought about that meeting to learn what I had learned about my brother. I knew that catching him then, on the trolley, and catching him unposed was the only way of knowing his inner painter's view. He did not much reveal with words of the English language or with visible demonstrations of his body the warmth he harbored. He did not know how to be gracious or sociable. He was awkward in his spirit and private to such a degree that he did not care about social niceties. But in the moments of our serendipitous meeting he was loose, and listened to the master, watching and fully aware of the power of the canvases around him. The only way to know him was to catch him in that poised moment, while he was following his own star. You could not know where that star was taking him. You could only sense that he had has own precious star, and if you caught him walking (so awkwardly) or gazing (so intently), you could see his getting there.

Once in the melee of the summer moon, we went for a boat ride on the low-created waves of calm Lake Erie. It was hot, so hot that the air shimmered with alluring reflections from the water. We had taken off a few hours from work in order to be down by the shore before the sun set. Once the boat was ready to sail, we left Colchester Harbor on a port-side tack, drifting easily along with just the mainsail and a blooper. Half way down the coast towards Bar Point, we dropped sail and decided to go for a swim in the pea-green little sea.

As we swam around the boat, the foredeck painter slipped off the bow and into the water. Janine grabbed the painter with all the aplomb of an experienced sailor and began hauling on the line, while treading water. Soon the boat started to lurch through the water in her direction. Then, Janine started swimming with the line in her hand. Her motions were tense, jerky, difficult. After some experimenting, she found that it was easier to move with her entire body under water, and she dove like a deep-sea fish, taking the line with her, holding it under her left armpit, wrapped around one arm. Then, as she swam, the boat obeyed her command, and her motion was easy, serene.

We swam like two porpoises, slim and efficient under water, rising every 20 feet to the surface for a long gulp of air, then back under the Lake Erie wavelets, she with painter in tow, neatly stowed under her left armpit, towing the boat. I fantasized that Janine was a porpoise, glistening through the waves in her light green bathing suit, as well adapted to the waves as any porpoise, and smoothly efficient in her tugging, towing, woman-boat-handling maneuvers. Even her arms had the graceful movement of fins; her legs had the power of a tremendous tail-back shark, her hair streamed back and shook in the water. I decided then and there that I loved her more than any other creature alive, any creature I could imagine or contemplate or see or foresee.

On another passage out from Colchester, we rollicked along on a fine brisk breeze, with just our Saturday, day-sailing supplies: a few quarts of liquid refreshment, a few oranges; a few ounces of fine cheese, and a windbreaker in case of night return. The ride was so fast, so unexpectedly peaceful and adroit that we just kept sailing, Southwest on a beam reach toward Pelee Island. Half way there, at the point where the freighter channel crosses the direct route to Pelee Island, we started to talk about staying the night on Pelee Island. It was, at first, a fantasy. Janine and I had never stayed overnight on the Island. We would not be prepared for it: no fresh clothes for dinner, etc. However, as we scudded along, the temptation of leaving our mainland cares behind overwhelmed us. and we kept the boat on course for Pelee Island when the late afternoon hour would normally have dictated: Time to return to home port.

Once ashore at Pelee Island, we took our precious little gear in a knapsack up the hill to the Algonquin Inn, where we would, unannounced, spend the night. Janine was not prepared for roughing it on the boat; and I was not about to treat her to a memorably uncomfortable first night out on the boat. So, up to the Algonquin Inn we went, with a knapsack of old fruit and stale water but no toothbrush, no change of underwear.

The journey home was more eventful. The peaceful little Lake Erie bathtub was kicking up five- to six-foot waves. The wind was blowing a steady 30 knots, gusting to 40 knots. Just getting sails up in a stiff wind is a challenge in a small day-sailor, like our 21′ O'Day Mariner. There are no winches, so the sails must be positioned perfectly to take the wind on the nose, or the power of the wind in the sails will pull you immediately off luff-position and make it progressively harder to raise the sails over the last span.

Furthermore, the only safe way to position oneself to operate the halyard in a stiff breeze is in the cockpit; and from that position, the crew cannot get a good foothold for hauling down the halyard. But the halyard must be hauled down hand over hand, with great speed if you are to raise sail before the wind catches it and alters your position. Helmsman and crew must cooperate so that the helmsman keeps the bow of the boat positioned directly into the wind by making fine adjustments in the motor's angle of attack, while the crew raises sail. Timing and communication are of the essence. We succeeded this time, although we did not always manage a smooth transition from motoring to sailing.

On a day such as this, you recognize that tough conditions call for fortitude and determination. You recognize that sailing is not always the smooth picture-book image that your summertime cruise operator's brochure makes it out to be. In heavy wind conditions, you must simply decide to take the waves, one at a time, and adjust the helm with the rise and fall of each crest. You watch the weather with an eye to adjusting sail, or reducing sail, if need be. You set your compass course to get to your destination, and you make good on it, minute by minute. There is nothing more to it than that: patience and determination.

But your crew, your crew may be a little faint of heart, seeing huge waves towering over the quarter-bow, and feeling seasick after a period of hard-pummeling drops—one after another after another, with no human remorse and no hope of reprieve—into the troughs of the waves. Then the helmsman may experience a difficulty no conditions as sea can prepare him for—he may have a crew who wishes to mutiny or jump overboard. Then, the patience of the captain with his mate is truly tested. And, so was my patience tested on the return passage from Pelee Island with Janine.

She was not comfortable. She was not capable of sustaining any significant effort, under these adverse conditions. She wanted to be out of the sea-way and home. Patience was not her game to get there. Rather, she yelled and criticized and took out her fury at the weather on me. My thoughts were concentrated, first on getting the boat safely home, then on making her comfortable. She could not rile me. I was a rock in the waves and she leaned on me.

At long last, we pulled into Colchester Harbor. There, everything changed. We could leave our idyllic passage, our swimming, our love-making and our laughter behind. Janine knew that something had changed when we landed. I was less attentive. I was less focused on her.

But the romance of our passage held sway for a long time. I had found her. I had wooed her. I let her know that the loveliness of that passage was the most meaningful thing in my life.

The loveliness of our experience together on the water and in the water was part of a seamless flow of music, like the sound of water flowing over a dam or a high gorge. We changed the venue. We changed lakes. The wind changed on us. And still, the flow of the water was endless; the sound of the flow was music to the soul, tingling high, reverberating low, constantly shifting as our own moods shifted, constantly seeking new pathways to the jagged cliffs below. That music is still billowing the sails of my soul in that lost water of endless passage. The music sounded something like this:

She dove like a fish
Delighting in her own mischievous form,
Tight, in her green little bathing suit,
Sleek with her long-legged dorsal fin,
Gracefully placing every movement
with the care of an acrobat on the high wire;
Powerfully pulling, moving the bowline
through the water, under her arm,
with all the practiced experience of a long-
shoreman tying up a tanker, she,
like a mermaid fit for the sea, practiced
her movements for all the fish to see.

And when the stroke was done, the boat moved,
galloped a couple of feet on the lapping
waves, tagged along gamely, smartly,
delighted in its own gurgling way,
as it swallowed the waves and followed my mermaid
exactly where lady led it to go.

And I, helpless beside the hulk,
and marveling at the strength of every stroke,
kept my counsel in the gurgling water
and watched her dive and pull, stroke
and pull again, then let the air
out. How could words reveal
something more than she herself
revealed of grace, and transmutation?
Like a mermaid she did dive.

NOTES OF A BEACH-WATCHER

A long lanky fellow in a traditional boxer-cut pair of swimming shorts walks down to the beach at Colchester at the end of a Saturday afternoon. It is close to 6:00 p.m. and he is obviously tired from a day' s work.

On joining his family at the beach, he proceeds to scatter several handfuls of bread, one smidgen at a time to the pigeons. He seems to enjoy the company of the pigeons. He seems intent on feeding them, as though they were his own baying hounds.

These wilds birds wait for the hand of their master to spread the good food. They wait patiently, but still cackle at his slow painstaking ways. They like to be around a human being with such considerate hands, and such considerate ways.

Then mister from the upper beach turns his attention to his wife, sitting quietly on the blanket some few yards off from where the pigeons now evaporate. Mister sits down beside her. He talks a few minutes, she nods her head. Then he begins to rub her back, using broad, back-and-forth full hand motions. She responds; she shimmies her back in happy response.

Finally, she mellows out, relaxes every muscle, and lies calm, in happy harmony with the energy from his hands.

The man from the upper beach then lies down, stretching his muscles, and breathes long draughts, deeply, in and out. He lets the sun warm his belly and warm his head. He rests quietly without moving any part of his body for a few minutes. Then he is ready to go for a swim in the Great Lake.

PETOSKEY STONES

DARK LAKE,

inky black, discolored
by remains of ash
and beech and paper birch,
This ledge of water sits
immovable, tight, secure
against the future, trapping
every particle of mountain
past, reflecting every
ashen face that ventures
from the two-pronged night
and moves not a shimmering second
to simulate the light,
vacation-splattered lakes.

The stillness and the black
attract a wary driver
rounding the curve of a Northern
dusk: This dark immobile
water lies in wait
for the headlit traveler stumbling
along at freeway speeds
and arrests him feet-first, head-
in-the-clouds, rain-on-his-shoulder,
hands-go-free until

he smartens up and finds
a way to replace that nar-
cissistic bottle in the car
with a presence on the mountain
ledge, which, like a paper birch,
reflects his essence, clear, serene,
and scrolled to dip in the inky lake.

POEM

As a water droplet severs off the mass
of falling water-sheets, blue-green and smooth,
falling church-wall-thick over the lip
of gray Niagara's ancient limestone mass,
so each of us (established, breathing, born)
glints off the common gene pool, deep and quick,
and sails a day by windsight, lone and lofty,
then merges with the church-wall 'neath the rock.

We think we know the direction of descent
and steer with oars and rudder bent to the wind
but when the magical wind has played her tune
we see a curve in the direction of becoming
which shows a beauty no one could have known,
least of all the droplet on the eve of falling.

PRAYER TO THE UNIVERSE

Oh Lord, I pray that I shall not miss the main
event: cuddling with you each close of day
Digesting tidbits of gleaned meat from the rack
Of daily travels, fed the Eskimo way.

Knowing that our love shall pale the setting sun,
I know our closeness can survive these wayward
Moments of exploration, just as now
We love, despite my dense diversions backward.

If love is the candle leading us through the valley,
You are my candlestick: I'll hold you tightly
'Til the candle burns my hand and then let's see
If we are melded, walking side by lightly-

Stepping side, reading children's stories
From a common light. And then if not,
My prayer will still be sending signals, dream-
like, wise, insistent, a prayer to hold us taut

To one another. Now in the morning mist
I say a daylight prayer to bring us close,
To cast out to the hundred million suns
My hope that all the fibers of connoted

Meaning will connect our distant love
And draw you to me for the main event;
And let not you nor I forget our great
Concordance. Let us draw beneath the tent.

ST. LOUIS BLUES

My woman's done been gone a long time now
She can't comprehend how I would risk
Life's happiness flat for a dive with the fish
But after the scare is scattered, she went South
And I got stuck with lots of wonder-stones
Walking the walk, without a horn to blow.

Gone beneath the good times, took a leave
Like a flock of geese in winter, flown
To warmer cornbeds, sheltered, lonely
She did stray, cribbed in a dry creek
While I was threshing miles of wonder-stones.

See that beauty, that gray and emerald good-time
Stone? I showed it to my mommy
Way back when I had it, show-
And-tell to all my spirited schoolmates, time
When I could walk the walk, with horn to blow.

My horn, a schoolboy's pride, would hold a tune
(However out-of-tune) to turn
The ear of a jay, a crow, a worm
And bear my pride on the hand-held air. I crooned
As I skipped and turned the piles of wonder-stones.

That special beauty, emerald all too fine
I rolled down the beach and round the back
of silly consciousness (Wendy's crack
attracts me like no other lover's) so
I walked that walk, having no horn to blow.

The emerald washed in a torrent of gotta-be's
Down and out to the common sea,
Effluvia merged with the mortgage, the degrees,
The washed out dreams in a flood of tears: who knows
The reason why nature gives you wonder-stones?

My woman long-time gone—so long I wonder
Where her heart is among the stones—
Come back now, brave and beautiful, slumbering
With the power of tides, rolling my weary bones
Along the winding beach of wonder-stones:
I walk that walk, with love's sweet horn to blow.

GUARDIAN OF THE AIRPORT

Serenely situated above the traffic,
feathers cocked below the wire,
Red-tailed hawk surveys the scene,
master of all that flies or tries.

The traffic doesn't slow to notice
(as they do for accidents)
but moves to the groove of commuter-blues:
Get there on time and without dents.

The guardian of the airport telescopes every
dimension of the visible universe inside
his feather-crowned bird-brain: what he computes
from dense and deep-dish images we find

of no interest. But the heraldry
of Red-tails with their under-fleece
of white, fringed high above with russet
is told a hundred-fold in these

Sharp-imaging eyes. How will commuters
fare in half a billion years?
Will we encrust the planet with extreme
excrement and veils of acid tears,

Will the genes of *Buteo Jamaicensis*
transmute in frigid air to something
strange and far removed from original
time; will we hold the sun's transit

As the patrimony and the sacred gift
of our collective stewardship; or will
we consume the air on the ship? Have we
forgotten: The guardian of the airport wheeled

Above the jet-way when it was slime
by the side of a forest? Perhaps we care
too much about being at the gate on time
when studying the habits of the hawk would get us there.

THE BLOOD OF THE BIRD

Once was your wing adept at crossing roads
to eat the carrion left by other drivers;
now its structure is lost upon the wheel
and little bird bones gather for a meal.

My driver friend believed behavior would be
governed by experience, **his** experience
with other crows in native Georgia, distant
by two thousand miles, distant by
a change in culture, habits, inter-relatedness
with people in a rural culture.

No. The blood was crimson, glowing, as it passed
our point of view, flying in a windstorm
past the rules of Georgia conduct, shorn
of future past or present purpose, clasped
no more to the motion of the earth, save
to gather karma for a resting place.

COMING AND GOING

When eyes behind the doorframe flew
to the open window, there to behold
the great diversity of creatures strewn
About the sky, the trees, the garden,
through each pool, across each strand,
My brother's eyes grew big. He said:
Stay, my Savior, dip to hold my hand;
His Gracious loveliness now slips beneath the bed.

Between our rooms we greet one another
Sorrowful, angry, glad, or afraid
in the space where a door is not enough
to define the human meeting place.
We sometimes miss our lines of transit,
and make our exit or our entrance
unannounced, but always smiling,
His Gracious loveliness upon our lips.

Between the actress and the act
of sex are many feckless sighs
of great or feigned relief: suppose
her husband does not know how high
is high, how low is low on madam's
finely tuned clitoral scale?
Poor man must find salvation, asking,
Stay, my Savior, dip to show my hand.

Then, too, we many times have friends
who claim to be undying buddies,
but they have ego-needs to feed
and find your friendship is a graceful
vehicle upon life's highways, greatly
admired by others in authority,
as are camellias starting in the gardener's shed.
His Gracious loveliness now slips beneath the bed.

Frightened, come the final hour,
Every mortal person stalks
his bygone years to find the flowering
moment that cannot be undone;
My brother made a flower or two
of wondrous beauty, solid, fired-sand,
now rotting in the rain behind his tomb.
Stay, my Savior, dip to hold my hand.

So as we gather near to find
the meaning in our family rites
each member turns to ask, if I
might be of service to your plight.
But when we reach the empty chair
there is no service asked, no hand
to hold; no place to plant the kiss.
Why was he here, Lord, if not to share?
Stay, my Savior, dip to hold my hand.
His Gracious loveliness now slips beneath the chair.

WALKING ON THE BEACH

Whistling down sunlit groves
Bemused by spring in the fearsome
Folly of autumn's desire
(Driven by the Great Lake winds
On a blowzy coastal cove
Around the crotch of ancient
Oaks) my Fairweather's chief
Delight is walking—briskly;
No minced words, no waste;
Determined in the brittle breeze
To make the point of prominence
Then hustle downwind back
To the grove of quaking aspens.

How would it be my companion
May or may not be;
Is walking sadly by my side
Preoccupied in spirit;
Would or would not be
Delighted in my company,
Withdraws to wantsome thoughts
Of John-dear's needy lot
Sashaying left and right
Along the roaring beach,
No pathway picked or reached.
How would I be here, close
And frozen, with this woman?

Fair-weather says forget
The stormy past, review
Each fair new wind for purpose;
Find a path that meets
Your gait and stay the prickles,
Stay the changes. Around
The point, the sands shift slowly
And the wind shifts quickly, dumping
Human purpose in its way.
Then can you use the auto-
Pilot, having set the course
To the farthest point, reset
To the grove and the watching oak.

WALKING ON CLOUDS

I walk in scallimuffin clouds
along a fine and narrow street
dawdling inwardly, hurrying
the beat of my workaday feet to find the town's

beat. Once in the pyramid of power
downtown (bankers, lawyers, publicists
convene in frenzied word and blissful
dollar bleeps) I start my shower

of words, the formatted, fully controlled
deluge of persuasive prose, read once
by a clerk and a regal audience of one.
This is the way the law unrolls.

We walk our inimitable ways
along the smooth and winding street
while bleating, braying, cooing, speaking
in the tongues of man to make a trail,

a cavalcade of sound within the dark
and winding road, we walk the walk
because we got up early, socks
on both feet, ready, willing, far

from any destination. What ho?
Isn't that to walk in clouds
degraded from an inner shout?
Where do you come from; where do you go?

VILLANELLE

In Jesu's heart, He reveals His sacrosanct goal
Writ large on the freeway overpass no traveler could miss,
Unless you're surfing the FM radio.

For travelers with heart, the way is clear, the going
Slow as befits a roadway slick at Christmas.
In Jesu's heart, He reveals His sacrosanct goal.

As we commuters gather in the fold
of urbanopolis, we hear what we want to miss
Because we're surfing the FM radio.

That sound competes with the voice of the inner soul
Beamed quietly from imagined streetlights, fixed
In Jesu's heart, He reveals his sacrosanct goal.

The sound, the sight of godliness can roll
into a big ugly bear when the images shift
As when you're surfing the FM radio.

Turn off the noise and hear the roadway's low
Sweet hum, below, above, singing a hymn.
In Jesu's heart, He reveals His sacrosanct goal,
Unless you're surfing the FM radio.

COLCHESTER HARBOUR: TABLEAU IN SEPTEMBER

1. CHILDREN ON THE BEACH.

Delighted by sand fleas,
Bitten by courage,
Toddlers make and break castles on the beach.

2. SEA GULL IN THE VALLEY OF A WAVE

On misty green
Quiet as a stone
Herring gull rides coherent and at peace.

On darker days
In choppy seas
Herring gull whirls above the frothing fray.

3. GRANDMA IN THE SUN.

Laid back and relaxed
In the wrinkle-free canvas
Grandma folds her knitting just to chat

With Daisy, who's four.
She found first place
With Grandma, eyes and ears all holding forth.

4. FREIGHTER HULL-DOWN.

Slipping sideways,
Smokestack leading
Bridge in tiny steps beneath the waves,

This silent waltz
Records the curvature
Of the place where the ship and the dance all halt.

5. TEENAGERS IN A POWERBOAT.

Water swishing in broad bands
Faster than cocker-spaniel-do,
You know the child is father to the man.
Two strapping teens
Play hide and seek
With power at the helm of a sleek female machine.

6. SAILBOAT AT DOCK.

Both legs glistening
With generous oil
Both girls lie relaxed on poppa's rich

Ship, bedecked
With silvery spoons
Of various sizes and descriptions, naked.

7. THE COLOR OF THE SUN.

Late hazy day
Summer dwindling
In the breathable evening to a long-stemmed yellow

Lily; translucent
Purple in the clouds
Turn white to celebrate the mighty king's descent.

8. Fishing in the Lakes

In the bow of the *Bounteous*
Pussy, old man
directs all hands aboard in loops of countless

Stories; then
The anchor stowed,
He chugs to port, to drink, to market, and to bed.

9. Moon on the Masthead.

Cocked back to sail,
Relaxing on her back
Across the Zenith's blue, this shillelagh moon

Rattles her teeth
At mankind's blissful
Ignorance of natural processes.

10. Vantage Point: Colchester Harbour.

From where do I see
These pithy scenes
Of young and old; at work; at play? I reel

My fish from the shoals
Around the lighthouse,
Winding the season's memories fast and close.

THE VIRTUOSO
for Itzak Perlman

Who knows what sting of the asp
inside his fiery head
set technical virtuosity
to spinning around Saturn's edge.

With loss of one faculty
a person sometimes finds
compensatory super-acuities
and talents honed by time—

enforced development. Others
find, with no visible loss,
their talents bloom by force
of habit, spinning gold from dross.

And, common to all is the feat
of learning to tie your shoes;
it takes a few days or a week
to see the business through.

Thus armed with precedent,
we know true learning takes time
and practice, getting the muscles
tuned so the stroke is sublime.

It's when the artist goes
beyond the precedent
to dazzle even himself
that learning has served as the bed

of inspiration's bloom.
And yet such dazzling tapestry
of sound, of texture, movement
up and down the registry

of violin sounds moves floating-
slowly, by galactic measure,
from the edge of the bow, from the edge
of the horsehair to human treasure.

EMANATIONS FROM A HORSECHESTNUT TREE

(with apologies to Wallace Stevens)

I

How many ways can a tree
establish human importance?
Or does it matter, looked at
solemnly, squarely from a view
two millimeters from the leaf?
One chestnut first appears
the same as others, rooted
in residential sewers,
revealing frilly white
napkins, tres petite,
on wavable, billiard-green
tablecloths for a queen.

But each tree has its shape
its special notch or fork or cleft
in the lip of speaking to the sky:
One tree is balanced towards
a house, the next is ramrod
straight, a third is straggled
a little left, a little right.

An eight-year old who studies
trees sees very different
meanings in each branch.
Two trees are not alike.
Two eight-year-old boys are not alike.

II

Of course, there is the fruit,
the gene-transmitting pea
in the pod, or here, the walnut
hard Horsechestnut housed
in a thickle-thorn shell of spikes.
One curious boy, so long
ago decided to find
the heart of the chestnut pea
and took a stumpy kitchen
knife to torture the nut
from the shell, but found its hardness
deflected the blade to his thumb.

Cut to the bone and bleeding—
off to the stitching-room, sewn and bled of tears—
how hard, how very hard strikes back
the nut of a different species.

III.

This spriggy boy, my brother,
and I played war on the street
with wagonfuls of chestnuts aimed
in slingshots at the brazen feet
of marauders from the next street.
A well aimed chestnut bullet
left a super-sting
and raised a black and blue
for many weeks to see.
How could he—two years
my junior—know they were hard:
Chestnuts were not steaks
or butter to be slithered with a knife.
He had to learn in a way
I could not know he had to learn,
two years his senior.

IV.

Layer after layer of sunlight
hard on the lap of chlorophyll
directed to the sun
unleashed boundless leaf-
and fruit- and juice-making energy.

Love laid on its back
caressing legs and arms
with juice of the inner fruit
unbundles millions of pixels,
puts new face on old pictures.

V.

A ponderous wifely ass
wide and waddling on the tarmac
(crouching low to feed
the scavenger Canada geese)
creates a rearranged circuit
in that place in the brain where Cheney
Wildlife Refuge and
those wandering lascivious geese
all say: My wife and I were here.

VI.

But how to visit those memory
graveyards, fresh and filled
with New World enthusiasm, that
is the question. Today's new female
may well become tomorrow's
antiquarian relic.
Yet here today is here today:
One cannot get stuck
in the relish of yesterdays.
Perhaps if you go by the nose
or the sight or the swell of that inner

curve to its inmost quiet
fulmination, you'll know
the circuits can be overlaid,
the signals crossed from daybreak
to previous nightfall, the brain

enriched so deeply, these
new labia become a history
lesson, teaching dumb
humble me in the nameless glory
of their wordless smells, their endless story.

VII.

Would the whippoorwill grew as stout
as that old remembered chestnut tree:
the sound in the woods in the evening air
of such a bird would break the bonds
of memory from the tying post
where pain was dished out daily, strangely,
never to be forgotten, but only
just remembered, just ripped open
in the flush of new experience.
(The sound of the bird in the wood forty
years later is just the same, but freshly
felt with tears on the face or sweat
in the groin, which the child of six knew not.)
Without that tying post, where
would a heart of forty summers' flight
come back to call its home? Where
would a man brushed and gussied up
with luscious, rich, and trying travels
go to make a quiet peace
with his inner heart, his heart's first fruit,
if not to a place where pain is remembered,
love was revealed and the whippoorwill sang,
strong, unseen in a bare soft breath?

BLIZZARD IN THE CITY
(January 19 & 20, 1994)

Whipping wind,
sharp city corners;
snow drove sideways
curbstone high by quitting;
legs in stockings freeze to the bees' apple crotch;
men in tweeds
sloshed to the jerk-me-off socks
parade in weather fit for penguin kings.

Now rolling homeward
on ice and steel and modern
engineering,
no amount of which can stop
the arctic onslaught
or deter the gross invasion
of electronic nerves—
the great American machine
is close to helpless,
swishing in the lubricant snow.

Fractured nerves allowing,
driver notices the wholesale
transformation
(landscapes turned to moonscapes)
inherent in, building,
driving the blizzard's beat.
How else poor driver's
roadmap stay on course,
but beauty behold
each turn, each blessed foot.

Descending steeply,
cascading through woolly snow,
a siren signals
urban distress of heart;
Emergency transit
can't move faster than the fastest
car can move aside
(windblown claxons
clanging the silent snow).
These ripe commuters
wrestle inner stiffness,
battle mind-
fatigue to hold the road,
to keep control
of famously complex systems.
Only delicious
honey-dew smells propel
a flagging spirit
down love's private highway.

Why the battle?
Weather is one condition
the planet abides.
Conditions at the Pole last week
determine wind
and snow: love at the end
of the road or end
in a drift, awaiting life-
support, love's siren
lost in the wailing snow.

PHONEMES

1. Words are the source,
words are the source, all right,
of all misunderstanding.

2. When a man and a woman talk
the birds blink twice to think
this might be another way to fly.

3. Shapely snow
late winter
early morn
descending but not holding
to the surfaces of the city;
but holding to the shelf
of the bronzed municipal breasts,
for all the world
two castles adorned
in shapely snow.

4. Peel back the orange rind
thick and juicy;
Do this slowly
and with grateful precision
if you want to taste the core fruit.

5. "Daddy, can we play
some putt-putt golf?"
"Shush, Susie, I'm on the phone."
And the big black Mercedes
turned the corner before
I could hear the daughter's reply,
if any.

What do you say to a man
who has it all
and does business from the car
on the way home, when

he has his daughter's rapt attention,
now 'til home;
nine years old to when;
security figure to lost intimate.
What do you tell such a man,
if anything?

6. WHAT AM I SUPPOSED TO THINK
when we make love, you turn away,
you stretch your back to the setting sun.
What am I supposed to feel
when you come home, lips red and lipstick
pinched to a tuck around your shirtsleeves?

Am I supposed to think you're bored
or just tired?
Am I supposed to feel forgiving or just bemused?
These changes presage death, my love,
but surely you will leave the premises
for you know as well as I do
where I keep the gun; and who—
Do you suppose that I know how to use it?

7. FLEECE OF SNOW
clinging like booties,
baby sweaters
to every roof and chimney,
Fleece of snow
blesses my southern view
from the 34th floor.
late spring, each roof
from the 34th floor
is a postage stamp
bearing the town
to a new destination,
through the fat of the year
and the unknown gales.

MR. VINAL RETURNS TO MCDUCKY'S FAST BEAUTY TREATMENT LANE

(with apologies to e. e. cummings)

Drive right on through, Mr. Vinal,
Don't take a napkin; don't leave a wrapper;
we'll pick up after you, just like Mom did.
The service battalions of the biggest franchise
in the Mother-consuming, almighty bucko world
have no fear of your fetid smells or left-over
cheese-dip skins. We get paid for this, they say,
and smile all the way to the vinyl garbage can,
(and so does the sanitary engineer smile,
all the way to the downtown bank).

It really doesn't matter what you want:
is it for your car, or for your face,
or for your Mom or for your date ?
We have a fast food place a few blocks away,
in this brave land of plenty, Mr. Vinal,
that'll serve anything you want,
just drive right on through, Mr. Vinal,
do not pass GO, do not collect
two hundred dollars or any other token
of you're having played the Board.

If you want a home cooked meal, why
we can order that up, too, on wheels
(if you like) or served in bed
or diced up neat on a blue china plate.
The cookin's good, but you cannot get a nibble
of the cook-mate's nipple no matter how you cry;
she (or he, as the case may be) has other
customers to serve: the body must be clean
for this sweet job, and baby finger contact
is not within the job description, sorry.

But if you drive on further down that alley
There's a service station for the body
where they hardly touch you; you'll enjoy
the swift message, the sweet perfume, Mr. Vinal,
it's not much different than a drive-through wash.
I've been there myself a couple of times. I come.
I smile. I drive on through. I hit the road
refreshed, relaxed, and ready for another
hard day making big bucks at the track
where no one slows down except to bury the dead.

And then, the scent of the newly ripened earth
alive with the rain is not enough to stop
the hum-hellion ride to the next service stop,
to feed the next-spoken need of body, face
(drive-through doughnuts, prayers to God).
But, Mr. Vinal, I'm sure you'd rather
drive right on through without a pause for napkin, grace,
For if you stopped that long, you might just wonder
Who picks up the garbage here ? And if I'm not
completely satisfied, can I talk with Alice ?

ONE TO GROW OLD ON

Whatever sound you sing
To leave the blues behind
Let Shiva dance a shimmy
Longside Gatemouth Brown
To give true shape to madness,
And make a wave for memory's
Curling iron to save.
Then press your blues to the bottom
Of your barrel-headed horn and beat
That daddy eight to the bar.

Home leaves lotus
Whispering out-of-doors
Like rain on wicker-roofs
Leaves behind footprints,
Thumbprints, many little
Digit prints. Such
Are a mother's memories, never
Cast in clay or stuck
In hoppin'-the-beat bleating words,
But still, like rain in a gale.

INVITATION TO DANCE

My daddy, me oh
will you dance with me?
This Latin cha-cha sung
in thirds and thirteenths high
above the mandolin
tells me through the ground beat:
time to rise and dance.

All the other diners
in this snug paesano
restaurant sing with gusto;
holding hands to their hearts,
they belt out every chorus.
Some fellows tuck their bellies
in and take the floor
to rattle every beat
and twirl on the downbeat;
make the cha-cha something
strong and manly tender,
sweet as a rose at midnight.

Other dancers shimmy
sideways, bending backward;
reverse and reel forward;
dance silently (like the play
of line upon the steelhead
trout) while standing still,
frigid, dancing inside
out without the trout.

If only you would join me
for your favorite dance
(I mean get up, get out
and move the body to the bone)
I know we'd make a memory
deserving of our love
(a place to hold the skeleton
mercilessly close to the throne).
Then, besides the strength
and wisdom, the bough, the thorns,
the tender budding shoots
I'd know I shared with you
the rose at midnight while
we cha-cha'ed smoothly
to the mandoliner moon.

CHRISTMAS EVE

The images of a dozen years
go by on Christmas eve
accumulating speed
just like a world-class racer's
tour upon the mountain.
Each crossroad semaphore
the shape and size and color
of which assumed significance
the days I raced that mountain
merge in rapid sequence
on the long road down. One color
becomes the beacon within.

In many quarters Christmas
slows the pulse of men
and women trained to achieve:
We slip back to the fun
of being children, moment
to moment awake, not striving
for effect or gold stars
but to roll the ball
around the kitchen corner.
There, I remember the color
of the ball; the shapes we signaled;
the push our eyes gave the ball.

In many quarters Christmas lights reveal a playful
spirit, wrinkling his nose
behind the house, along
the street, above the rooftops.
St. Nic plays on every
wickerwork front porch
in Tuscaloosa and shimmies
over every dome in Nome.
Now wouldn't you, dear child, enjoy a midnight ride
in his one-horse open sleigh?

A dozen years ago
or twenty: doesn't matter
if the season sings.
The playful lights of Christmas
blink in recognition,
when, remembering a friend
you cannot touch, the joy
is further back each season.
Oh let my bike race on,
dear Santa, paced by your gathering sleigh,
and guided my moonlight, blue or green.

IN THE LOOKING GLASS
(with apologies to T. S. Eliot)

The neighbors watch him come and go
talking of Feiffer, Miles, Trudeau,
beneath the breath of every step
muttering, reflecting on the mess.

There is security in his effects—
their order, neatness, cleanliness.
And in the vestibule he chooses
thoughts to match the place and move

beyond the street, the saw-toothed hound
of greed. He finds there tucked in the sound
of his voice returning home, the measure
of fineness, clarity, inner treasure.

As footballs cross the inner sanctum,
tones reverberate in tandem
from the wall, the hearth, and synchronize
their energy like one struck tine.

So much the artist, so much at home
that when he stops, the pen moves slowly
across the threshold of the past
(forward or back) defining a task

Of discovery, process, piece-work. Now
the moving pen describes a house,
the artist's home, and how he got there.
In the heart is his desk, cluttered with lots

Of paper projects; a calendar, outdated,
retained for its picture of a schooner (rated
ocean-worthy) and a water-color
from another life, his wife once painted.

On either side of the current clutter
are piles of neatly bailed fodder
for future projects, the writer's truth-
in-lending for the bank of the dead. The loose

disorder of this space prefers a much more
stolid order. The pen keeps circling
like a raptor doing dizzy swoons
above the roadside kill of a tourist.

This tourist, stranger, voyeur in these parts
could just as well be my neighbor, rallying
home and tired, ready for the re-runs
after a hard day's blinking at his cultural icons.

I, however, wait for the footfalls
to cease, sit on my bed and breathe
the deep sweet air of galactic concentration,
wait for the thin pure line of gyration.

A PETROGLYPH OF HIS OWN CHOOSING

You glide to the walls of invisible earlier presence:
Ottawa braves stood high in steady canoes.
By pressing ochre and fat to the greenstone canvas
They described the roving spirits in their woods.

Today you may or may not see the wavy
Red above the laptop level of the lake.
But be assured for many years this map
Will draw the backwoods loners through the lakes.

What will they imagine there above
The braves? The lines are mere discontinuity
Of color: Any animal can resurrect
Its image on the red or on the green.

The Rorschach of imagining is called to test
This canvas: Is it moose, or caribou, or hunters
Trained together, antler-spears pursuing
Phantasmagorical demons, deep in the woods?

There is no right and ready answer; study
Drives the animals towards the darker woods
Or drives the traveler to lean on his paddle, steady,
Calm, secure in the rhythm of repeated motion.

Pulling the bow 'round slow and steady to the current
Leaving images of backwoods ancestors, barren
On the greenstone cliffs, bereft of meaning (since
No human eye remains to read the text),

I ply the paddle with my traveling rhythm.
Only an afterglow of red-green caribou
Dazzles the placid lake, as sunlight shapes
A green-and-gold tiara on the shimmering blue.